Glitter Bomb

Glitter
Bomb

poems

Aaron Belz

A KAREN & MICHAEL BRAZILLER BOOK

Persea Books • **New York**

Persea Books, Inc.
277 Broadway
New York, NY 10007

Library of Congress Cataloging-in-Publication Data

Belz, Aaron, 1971–
[Poems. Selections]
Glitter bomb : poems / Aaron Belz. – First edition.
   pages cm
ISBN 978-0-89255-431-7 (original trade pbk. : alk. paper)
I. Title.
PS3602.E463A6 2014
811'.6—dc23
   2013042972

First edition
Printed in the United States of America
Designed by Rita Lascaro

For my kids

Contents

Glitter Bomb

A Novel

After a line by Molly Brodak

"Please write me a novel in which things are
wonderful in the future," said my new girlfriend,
then paused to adjust her skirt. She didn't realize
that I'm a stevedore and don't have a girlfriend
and besides, I live in Cleveland. I run a rat
show for the Ecuadorians while my invisible
butler serves them fake punch. It may sound
gimmicky but at least it doesn't pay the bills,
nor does it pay off the ducks that have those
bills still partly attached to their horrifying heads,
though I wish it would, because then I might
get clear of the jackass duck mafia constantly
on my tail.

"Please write me a novel," she began
again, as if already revising, "in which," but
then her words became soupy and depressing,
and besides, who really was she? At first I tried
to delete her from my phone, then called
a friend in Brooklyn at whose pad I'd crashed
not weeks before, and she suggested looking up
"girlfriend" in the Pictionary. So we began
communicating via hastily made drawings, first
of some dictators sitting at a bistro, outside,
in the springtime, one of them laughing,
saying,

"Write me a novel in which the undesirable
ethnic other has been purged," then the others
laughing too, and my Brooklyn friend guessed

"Hyundai dealership?" Uggh, I'm the rat man,
I can't draw, I want to make things wonderful
for both of us but wouldn't know where to start—

The Facial

I once had a friend who wrapped a towel around his head
and put slices of cucumbers on his eyes and reclined
and fell asleep and upon waking discovered
that he could not remove the slices from his eyes
and thus was for all intents and purposes blind
driven blind by his own perceived need for a facial
designed he had thought to remove dark circles
from his sagging bulging eyes that now were
he imagined dragon eyes for he could not see them
or even touch them with his fingers or Medusan
pure white eyes wreathed in snakes which in his blindness
he fancied to be a laurel commemorating his folly
a garland for his senatorial head banked in snowy drifts
of age or eyes that he himself had gouged out
with a shoehorn no kidding a shoehorn belonging
to his uncle a shoehorn he once played with deep
in an unfamiliar closet or the eyes of a Royal Canadian
Mounted Policeman peering deep into an underbrush
where a bandit had lately disappeared or even Japanese eyes
beautiful sad amandine head holes with majestic balls
in them balls now for all intents and purposes useless
and sometimes rockets brand new rockets aimed
out from his brain to the world to destroy with looking
everything they see so praise the Lord he thought
for technology and for fire and the ability to see
but that was imagination's limit for my friend
who had thought it would be nice to relax and
forget about life for awhile let the fruit do the work

Trees

I wouldn't go so far as to say
There's no such thing as trees.

Rhododendron

I spent an entire year refusing
to spell "rhododendron" correctly.
About six months in, I met a woman
who refused to spell "heinous" correctly.
Together we refused to spell "The
rhododendron is heinous" correctly.
This resulted in a relationship. But
I didn't know how long she planned
to stick to her resolution, and when
I asked her we had our first fight.
Eventually she broke things off.
I don't know where she lives now.

Your Objective

In a given situation
Your objective should be
To act as much like yourself
As possible. Just imagine
How you would act
And act that way.
A good rule of thumb
Is, try to be similar
To who you really are.
But keep in mind
That there's no way
To perfectly replicate
Yourself at all times.

My Chosen Vocation

When you emailed me
with news of my failure
in my chosen vocation
it left me confused
but also rather sexy-looking.

I slumped on the couch
in a daze, and my hair
was messy in an intentional way,
because I had volumized it
with Matrix Essentials
Foam Volumizer.

My beard was also volumized
with a vitamin enriched formula
that nourishes dormant roots
with essential nutrients
so that I looked like Walt Whitman
after he had walk'd along
the beach under the paling
stars of morning.

Song of Myself

As usual, I dined alone.
I went to pay the bill
and saw a printed sign:
"We don't split checks."

I told the woman at the till
that the sad and happy
parts of me wanted to
go Dutch today,

and could she make an exception?
She suggested, "Perhaps
the happy part could treat."
I said, "He's broke."

She seemed to understand
but still refused to split
the check. I stole
the toothpick dispenser.

So This Is Tuesday

So this is Tuesday.

So this—this is Pontiac LeMans.

This must be what they call
windshield wipers.

So this is Roddy Piper.

So this is macaroni.

This is what all the fuss is about.

It's Anchorage Alaska all
over again.

So this is elbow macaroni.

So this is K. D. Lang.

And this must be her left boot.

That would make this her right boot.

So this is what it feels like
to walk down the street, alone.

So this is the famous persimmon tree.

This is what Rowdy Roddy Piper
was telling me about.

So this is the most famous tree in Canada.

This must be what they call
"Margaret Atwood's Revenge."

So this is that hit single
by Michie Mee.

So this is what they play—
the DJs who can't see.

So this is the waste land
behind that one grocery store.

So this is what all
the swaying grass is for.

So this is my time sheet.

And this—this must be a very old ghost

come to tell me where to post

my time sheet.

No Vacancy

It's not that I'm uninterested.
I'm just *not interested.*

One way to spice things up
might be to send out for Vietnamese—

use those Swag Bucks
that have been dogging your wallet

like roaches. I mean, like roach
clips. Ever since the dam

collapsed it's been asps,
asps and a variety of wasps,

so who can really blame us
for, eh hem, "losing our touch"?

"Actually," they say.
"Let's be honest," they begin.

"On the flip side," I respond.
"As fate would have it," you admit—

you confess. "It wasn't *your*
fault," you continue, sounding

more like a marshmallow
with every swallow.

And as for the letter you addressed
to my head last summer,

I opened it this morning, and all
it says is "Hi." Cryptic much?

Interesting About You

What's interesting about you
Is the unique ways in which
You fail to distinguish yourself.

Team

There's no I in team,
but there's one in bitterness
and one in failure.

Ad Infinitum

Your best friend seems oddly familiar.
You've met before—but where?
Meanwhile, you're expending more
energy than ever in an attempt to appear

as normal as the people around you,
and those same people are doing their
best to act as though all that energy
means something. In the looking-glass

it's still you, plus what you've become.
That case you'd spent your whole life
gathering evidence to prove appears
to be faltering due to lack of evidence.

Its merits had rested in the charm
with which it had been argued, but
now the little bit of light that gleams
like evening flame in your eyes

can't be attributed to anything at all,
really. If it's beauty, it's disgusting.
If it's anger, it's even less interesting.
So you see yourself for what you are,

a kind of ever-setting sun—your
own life's most familiar error,
repeated in the company of those
you'd hoped would love you most.

1-0

I've taken a vote among
myself and it's unanimous
we'd like me to be slightly
less of a jerk if possible

given my busy schedule
we understand so whenever
I can get around to it
would be great thanks

The Clock

My grandmother
gave me a clock
before she died.

It was silver
and the chime
sounded like a cuckoo.

She said it was a
keepsake
to remind me
of our fun times.

Moments before
my grandmother
passed away

she sat bolt upright
in her bed and demanded
the clock back.

I was like,
"But Grandma!"
But no, she insisted,

she must have it,
it was foolish of her
to have given it away.

I gave her the clock.
She held it to her breast
and took her final breath

with a smile
on her face.
How precious

that clock must have been
to my grandmother—
almost as precious

as the moments
we spent together
before she died.

The Silent Life

Horse lilies are the festive kind
of shrub you like to throw at weddings
and other cadenced affairs for good luck

or just for fun, depending on what kind
of pontooning flibbertigibbet you are.

Some people who have lustrous hair
never even stop to think about their
need to wear lustrous shoes so as not to seem

out-of-balance,

yet you see them at these same affairs
treading dully on not only the horse lilies
but other people's feet,

drinking themselves to tears on brandy neat.

Thomas Hardy the Tank Engine

From now on my poetry
shall be like Thomas Hardy's—
I shall write about ponds
and about dying trees

and the sadness that creeps
into love, over time—
and that life is absurd
and death sublime.

And I shall be like Hardy
in the way that I think,
no longer contemplating
my kitchen sink,

its bottle of Dawn
and unwashed dishes—
instead, haphazardness
and lovelorn wishes.

But I shall not grow
a broad mustache
and wax it each day
into a flamboyant swash

or wear a starchy shirt
with its collar sticking up
or drink expensive tea
from an overly tiny cup

to emphasize how big
the head of an author
tends to be,
nor shall I bother

to refer to myself
as "the tank engine."
People already know
I'm a tank engine.

My Last Duchess

That's my last duchess painted on the wall,
Looking as if she were alive. She's not.
She was too flirtatious, so I had her killed.
Now I want to marry your master's daughter.

Palindromes

Hopkins Palindrome

I caught this
morning morning's
minion, then gushed
glossolalia thus:
"Suh tail a loss
olg deh sug neht!
Noinims gninrom
gninrom sihtth!
Gu aci!!'"

Famous Palindrome

My girlfriend has a freaking weird name:
Eman Driewgnikaerfasahdneirflrigym.

Two Utah Palindromes

Utah, I hatu!

We HATU, Utah. Ew.

Beginning with a Couplet from Jane Kenyon's
Boat of Quiet Hours *and Continuing with One from*
Jorie Graham's Region of Unlikeness, *Proceeding*
with Another Couplet from the Kenyon Book,
One from the Graham, and So on until the Last
Couplet, Which Is by Seamus Heaney (A Cento)

I was reading about rationalism,
the kind of thing we do up north.

Now I will make a sound for you to hear.
A sound without a mouth.

The sound of water rushing over trees
felled by the zealous beavers,

look up and it's suitors, applause,
it's fast-forward into the labyrinth

of my red dress with blue leaves
and lemon lilies—the one you bought for me—

sounds rising up now and then from the valley,
a hammering, intermittently a dog,

mid-afternoon the sound of weeping in the hall
woke me . . . hurried steps on the stair, and a door,

on the steps across the street a teacup of flour.
Three mismatched linen napkins folded below it—

the tiers of sugared pastries: angel wings,
cat tongues, and little kiwi tarts;

Let's consider the dark, how green it is.
Let's consider the green, how dark, with the rocker at its heart.

You are like a rich man entering heaven
Through the ear of a raindrop. Listen now again.

Indianans

When I arrived here I thought it was Indiana.
I discovered people and called them "Indianans."
I tried to convince them to become Christians.
I've since learned that this is not Indiana.

Eating Ice

Squire's omelet. Makeshift stew. Apple
hair. Nike treadnots. Spanishness.
Okee finokee. Boca Raton spittoon. Gloom.
Horace's finch cake. Spy novel. Degobah.
Lampwise by altarlight. Lunch spaghetti. Seed.
Cranmer's ignoble yet hip spendthriftiness.
Bellah. Macramé hog blanket. Eye razor.
Dracula marker? Toy billows? Blizzardly?
Ineptitude of Boris. Inordinate money.
Shame squadrons, elongated. Brillo fiends.
Aptitude reoriented toward symbiotics.
Phantom lace. Chain boy. Elf simony. Bees.
Crabbo. Zippo. Annie on the elephant tree.
Breech of doody. Lip horn. Grackle. Pi.
O gads. Utrecht's embarrassment. Andy?
Clear-skinned obese turnip farmers of yore.
The phantom. The pylon. The courtesan.
The baleful bondsman, old creep, eating ice.

Either / Or

Egg

Every animal
was born either by live birth
or by egg, I think.

Presidency

Every human being
is either the President
of the United States
or they are not. I am
told that there is
no middle ground.

Pregnancy

Every human being
is either pregnant
with another human
being, pregnant with
some other creature,
or not pregnant.
There is no "fourth
option"—so I am told.

Movies

Every animal either appears
in a major motion picture
sometime during its life span
or it does not. Which kind
of animal are you, Mr. Mountebank?

Arguing with a Buddhist

So yesterday I was trying to argue with a Buddhist,
but he refused to argue. He said we were both right.
I said that only one of us was right, and he nodded.

He said that we were both right and that was the end
of that, nothing more should be said about the matter.
It is not healthy to bicker in this way, he added.

I objected to his both-and reasoning, positing instead
my either-or logic, which I claimed to be sounder
and yielding of more fruitful philosophical interaction.

I said that if he truly embraced the both-and that he
would accept both both-and and either-or and not
insist exclusively on both-and. He said, ah, but

this is what I have been saying the whole time—
we are both right. I said, but you've foiled yourself
yet again: you cannot believe we are both right if you

continue to disagree with me. He said very well, but note:
it is you who are disagreeing with me, not I with you.
After that he gazed out the window for several hours.

And I could tell, just looking at him, that he was one.
The lamb chop exploded and macaroni headed pie-bin.
He gave out an eternal yes to any world that listened.

Starbucks

I love people,
and what working at Starbucks has allowed me to do
is get involved in people's lives.

A Yoking of Them Together

Berzo eats clams.
Minkse trades watches.
Barg waits tables.
Fengrove vomits.
Leppers begs to differ.
Trigger hates Finns.
Seamus collapses.
Zion elevates Susan.
Klee drips flattery.
Sven apes, spins.
Gerty spanks Barry.

Let me tell you what I mean by "Berzo eats clams."
It was at the wedding of Trigger and Barg.
And while we watched this racist marry a waitress,
Berzo was munching, Fengrove & Seamus drinking,
Klee complimenting Leppers against Leppers' wishes,
and Gerty and Barry in a coat closet making merry,
Minske trading watches, and the rest of them dancing.

Gerty spanks Barry.
Sven apes, spins.
Klee drips flattery.
Zion elevates Susan.
Seamus collapses.
Trigger hates Finns.
Leppers begs to differ.
Fengrove vomits.
Barg waits tables.
Minkse trades watches.
Berzo eats clams.

Gleff

I eat gleff. Seberi glomin eats gleff.
Kramer billious mown flags?
Yes, gleff. Spareny?

Mackris! The old fish of delliysm—
I do eat gleff. Sebery glomin does too.

The Tank

A willingness to jettison willingness in favor of jetties.

Some carob oil, some silk slacks, same sameness.

Sam at the tank: red paws, tiny fish chucked.

A wide vista varying from vague to very sharp.

Dawn in the dead sauna, down the dry bed: daytime

among these toothpick bones, rotten telephones.

Cast the white casket into cold white crashings

to see flappers flip in as we sip from capless canisters

among vague, very bright stones, speckled even.

Spotted deep in the black: Sam's image, full hands.

One Star

Of star-crossed lovers and cross-eyed lovers,
fate favors the latter; at least they're together,

even if they can't see each other's faces very well.
I once had a cross-eyed lover, back in Nam,

and I called her My Little Postage Stamp.
She called me Big Texas. We took breakfast

at the Viet Thanh hotel for a dollar each
then went down to the beach at Xuan Huong.

"I'd like to get away from earth for awhile
And then come back to it and begin over,"

I told her as she put Bain de Soleil on my back.
She shook her head and said, "Damn,

Big Texas, you make me laugh." We had
but one star in our never ending sky—lone

it hung over Xuan Huong, all day long
and into the night. My girl couldn't see it

on account of her sight, but I, in my mind,
kept voyaging there—and loving her more.

On the Loss of a Finger

There is no way to describe how sad
I was when I discovered my fingers
had fallen off. I mean, you find one
stub in the bed sheets—okay, you
can live with that. But three, four,
seven? And this morning, the tenth?
It was like when my toes fell off,
only worse, because I didn't use toes.
What are toes? But I had even named
my fingers: Edith, Marlene, Gretchen,
Bethany, and so on. Gwen. Ten
was named Marylou on account
of her inordinately diminutive size
and occasional bouts with dyspepsia.
When I found Marylou this morning
I laid her upon an unused limestone
soap dish in a shroud of serviceberry leaves
and sprinkled her in body powder
and prayed, then, for her quick ascension
through perdition, manual labor,
and through the finger puppet angels
up into her final glorification,
no longer tiny or sour-stomached,
but long, smooth, and incredibly sexy,
crowned with a perfect halo of a nail.

Michael Jashbery

I'm starting with the man
in the convex mirror.

Howard

Howard

Where there is a Howard, there is a

Howard

How is the "ard" of Howard. Take two Howards
And blend them into a large sugar bunny.
What you will find is that you now have one
Sweet sweet Howard. His name is Howard Cosell.
He died In 1995. He was seventy-seven years old.
He is not really named "Howard" now. He is called
"Jesus Christ," and he lives in infinity!

Howard

What is Howard?
Let us ask Howard.
Howard is everything
That isn't Not-Howard,
He says. Good grief!
My leather penguin
Could have told me
That. Oh sorry—*our*
Leather penguin.

Howard

Whenever I throw
A knife at the photo
Of Howard that hangs
In the dining room I
Miss badly and
Damage something
Expensive. Howard,
Howard, I'm moving
Your photo to your
Bedroom.

Howard

There isn't any Howard, per se.
He keeps his money in purse A.

Howards End

I once went to
Howards End.
It was spooky.

Trois Poésies Antiques

The Apple Orchard

When the apple orchard comes to eat you,
watch out: you don't want to be
eaten by an apple orchard.

Wack Kings

Watch out for the wack kings,
clanking their armor,
riding their dope horsies over the hill.

The Monkey Tuna

Do you love the Monkey Tuna?
Because I just ate the last of it.

An Enchanted Evening Together

Questions want to be asked.
Hence the question marks.
Such as: *How are you doing, Max.*
Max: *There are no meadowlarks?*

And: *Something is happening later?*
Symphony or symphonette—no.
Or: *No?* Not exactly French waiter,
but simplicity becomes you as you

become every question's worst answer.
What IS it about her? they moo.
You have the poise of a dancer,
but still, what *is* it about you.

A string part—a part for strings—
you play along on your air clavichord,
and so it wanders, fluttering its wings.
You order at last. *The soup du jour?*

We think thousands of things.

Hambone

Forced to analyze our relationship
I found myself thinking of it
in a completely old way.

You had a bonnet and a puffy dress—
Puff Mommy I called you (as a joke)—
and I a top hat and woolen britches,

and I was wiggling a bit,
getting into a fiddle concert
(town square, free for all ages).

"What hast gotten into thee?"
you asked. "I'm boogying!"
said I; "Why don't thou gettest

thy groove on, too?"
And you smiled a wan smile
and did a curtsy with a little

extra jiggle to it, and that one thing
madest my day. Then we went
to the general store and suck't

pickled pigs feet for awhile.
"Hambone," you said—that's what
you called me—"I likest thee."

Four Eights

"Introducing an altogether new way to Bounce!"

Wish I could log on
to what you're thinking about
right now. I wish my
earth-eaten shoes
didn't stink so much
of relish, too, and if beggars
were horses, wishes
would be Woad Raiders

soft-shoeing it through
darkling heaths to
your hut. Butt seriously,
Mrs. Attribute, where
did you get that television
remote? For my next
trick I'm going to guess
how many fingers I have.

Rain comes down
as parsley flakes sprinkled
unceremoniously on
spaghetti. In that tantrum,
we're the noodles.
You don't even know
which finger is
the most inappropriate,

can only guesstimate,
which means back
to the drawring board.
So much time, so little
to do! I only wish I
didn't taste like yachts—
in shorts, that I weren't
such a pasty little fellow.

Loggerheads

The people who used to rent carriages
in the late 1800s and the people who
invented the typewriter were at
loggerheads over the phrase
"carriage return." The former wanted
it for their signs at the airport
while the latter wanted it for,
you know the drill. I actually had a
friend in high school nicknamed
"The Drill" for his berserker-like skills
in a rugby scrum. He didn't even know
how to play rugby, but he'd hear that
"crouch!" Then, "touch!" And then . . .
I'm tired of existing on the face
of this planet. I want to live deeper in it
like Boris Karloff or Michael Jackson.
I've grown too fond of dreaming.
You know The Drill.

Naming Rights

Did we ever even call me that? There
isn't any evidence to suggest otherwise,
but also there isn't any evidence.

I'm not trying to pick a fight here.
I *am* trying to pick a bunch of other stuff,
though, such as a bone, with you.

That's the only thing I'm trying to pick
with you; the other stuff I'm picking
well enough on my own, such as my nose.

Let's dispense with the formalities
and get right to the elephant in the room,
shall we? Let's call him "Brass Tacks."

My uncle once part-owned an Arabian named
Brass Taxi. He raced in the Minnesota 1200,
faltered in the muddy stretch, coat full of foam,

big sad eyes; how I hate horse races
when they go on for a thousand plus miles.
What is this "winning" thing, anyway?

That's why I say I'm not here to compete
for naming rights, I'm cool, if that indeed
is what we used to refer to me as;

I just don't remember it, and one would
think I would, wouldn't one? One name isn't
another, nor is it necessarily "just as good."

Though I'm more and more okay with
Ahmad Malamud. Thanks, and I'll be seein' you
in the funny papers. Or just "around."

Aquatone Music

Tom, the aquatone music you sent
sounded like a jello harpsichord
played by an innocent but invisible child.

No, that's actually just a poet's lie.
The clear cassette you Fedexed
sounded like a brave studio performance.

But while we're speaking of it:
next time would you include
several of cousin Virginia's donuts?

They taste like stickybuns, or serum,
or whateveryoucallit—frozen gel.
When I see your picture I think of minks.

It's not professional to mention sundew!
No, that's a poetical comment. Here:
Send money. We are far from home.

Ice Cream

I scream, you scream, we all scream
when we get stabbed in the heart.

New Movie

The title of my new movie is *The Intern*.
The tagline is, "When ambition turns
into demon-possession..." Laura Dern

plays the part of a middle-manager
who's recently been diagnosed with cancer.
Lindsay Lohan plays a former break-dancer

who's been hired as Dern's new assistant,
her smile faint, her gaze distant,
she's inexplicably resistant

to doing any work. Turns out she'd rather eat
her coworkers in the break room—"meat
is meat" she growls, stuffing a pair of feet

in her tote. When Dern finally discovers
what's been going on she passive-aggressively hovers
around Lohan's desk until the two become lovers.

Gregory Peck plays the kindly janitor.
Jamie Lee Curtis plays Lohan's aunt (also a man-eater).
Tom Cruise is the town cantor.

Avatar

Blue computer graphics woman
with smooth cat nose, you are
purer, more in touch with nature,
and actually quite a bit taller than I—
and although you've discovered
that your soul mate is really just a
small, physically challenged white guy
gasping for air in a mobile home,
you've decided to stick with him.
I'd taken you for one of those shallow
pantheistic utopian cartoon giantesses,
but now I see that I was way off.

On the Death of Leslie Nielsen

When Leslie Nielsen was 27
he appeared in "Josephine,"
a play by Sally Benson.

So did my friend Orson Bean,
then 25 and also an
aspiring actor.

The year was 1953.
Together they toured
major cities,

including St. Louis
(they played the American),
Chicago, New York.

"That was my very first
Broadway play," Orson emails.
I show my BlackBerry

to my wife. "Wow,"
she says. (It's like the time
Allen Ginsberg called.)

"Surely Orson knew
about the death before you?"
I reply, "He says not.

And stop calling me Shirley."
But I can't do deadpan
the way Nielsen could. No one can.

Risibility Ballad

The preternatural
is sometimes risible,
especially when
it's partly visible.

Like when out steps
from bilious smoke
a wizard but
without a cloak—

only knickers
he is wearing.
That, and a
banana earring.

He looks like
Cecil B. DeMille.
He'd make you laugh
if looks could kill

and make you weep
if wands were ferrets
and you happened to be
allergic to ferrets.

So the extrasensory
reveals itself
as your magic joke book
glows on its shelf.

You chop the head off
your favorite bunny.
Well *that* trick worked . . .
but was it *funny*?

"Decidedly not—"
you smile wanly.
"Whatever happened
to Cyril Connolly?"

No one knows.
Nor do you.
You rise like smoke
through your own flue.

Hippie Slang

When I say
"I dig graves"
what I mean is
I enjoy and/or
understand them.

A Horse, Oh Gross

They called this a one-trick pony
As though that were a strike against it.
I said well it's only one strike against it,
And doesn't it kind of depend on what trick?
I have a horse that poops million dollar bills,
And that's really all it does, and you know what?

They called this beast Simon, or Sidoh; also
They called it Alice in Chechnya, which
I think was a reference to Alice in Chains,
And it was in this way that I began to see
The downside of having only one trick.
Man, that reporter's glasses were *thick*.

And we as Americans really have no idea
What's gone on over there even lately
Just as we as adults have no idea
Who's who in Halo or Zelda. It's ongoing.
It's the price we pay, and it seems reasonable
When it's peace of mind that's at stake.

Sergei Rachmaninoff

Doing stuff is fun, or it can be.
Sometimes it's more fun not to do stuff.

Vacation

We channel horseradish
On the daily vacation tab
It's kind of ridiculous
But people pay us for it.

I wish I could start again
Wiping my arrows clean
I've done it all wrong—
Somewhere the squid.

When it goes thump thump
I rally my faculties
Put on the goggles
And snap on the gloves.

Two cars are floating
Off through the reservoir
In one my darling
In the other my love.

We channel mayonnaise
With cocktail umbrellas;
So I keep a diary
And sleep on my back.

Big Face / M4W / Hollywood (Amoeba Music)

I think you noticed me ... You have a round face and rabbit teeth that you can't help but bare when you sniff. Your skin, stretched and shiny, appears to have been recently dermabraded. You have thick eyebrows that are partly, if not wholly, drawn on with magic marker. When I saw you, you were wearing tortoise shell frames inlaid with sparkly paste... no lenses in them (why, I may never know, but you are the demigoddess who decides these things) ... orange earrings and a seasick pea coat buttoned up to the throat, and it looked as though you'd lost your pants in a bet. You had a copy of *The Little Prince, Unabridged*, fat as a phonebook, tucked under your surreally skinny right arm, at the end of which dangled a stolen or inherited Vuitton purse, off of which jangled the keys to your convertible and your condo or apartment in ... somewhere stylish but affordable? (I guess that's why I'm taking the trouble to write all this.) I stood behind you in line and could not make out what you were buying, but it appeared to be Coldplay or Ingrid Michaelson or some other form of self-ingesting candy with which you perhaps enjoy feeding that evidently pulsing, sentimental, child's brain of yours. Mostly I remember your aroma which was super sweet and glamorous but come to think of it was laid on so thick that it might have been masking a rather more natural odor given off by your caricature of a feminine physique, my tulip, my honeycomb, O sticky bunch I long to drizzle lightly across the surface of the cold toast of this old man's heart. Let's meet up and you can tell me why no lenses, hey? Hookah out, or hit some thrift, perhaps? Or jam on some mellow tunez in your ride? I'll wait ...

Seven Habits of Highly Infective People

1. Be infected.
2. Leave open sores untreated and uncovered.
3. Spit or sneeze into other people's mouths.
4. Slice off part of your body and feed it to another person.
5. Vomit down someone's shirt, especially if they've recently had chest or abdominal surgery.
6. Tear off your face and wipe it (wet side-down) on someone else's face.
7. Cough without covering your mouth.

Tuberculosis Day

The acronym
we're going to use
for Tuberculosis Day
is TBD.

Mesquite Bar Code Squigglies

I made the mistake of reading Indian Barn
as a racist reference. Of course it wasn't,
and Aunt Coronary corrected me politely.
It was an artifact of antique Iowa and common
as a disembodied duck bill or a flugelhorn.
Perhaps this teaches us not to read
Indian Barn; just let it set there in the breeze.
(Aunt Coronary neglected to refresh these teas.)
Of the seven things exposed to breeze
in this psuedoaquatic environment, only one
begins with X and also ends with X,
and it's obviously not Indian Barn, but it's
important. I made the mistake of not learning
to spell, long ago, as a wee spry yearling.
Aunt Coronary's fireplace is flanked
with shelves bedecked with geodes and
barnacle, snapshots of hay bailers, statuettes.
The exposed thing could be a mattress;
it could be a tilting stack of flag stones.
But what it actually is is an X-large box
emptied of its contents: you fill it.
I pulled it out of yonder fuselage aflame.
Printed on it stylochronometrically: "Indian Barn."
I repaired it with homemade appleskin glue.
(Printed on me: a variety of tattoos.)

Wassily Kandinsky

No single terminology
really fits the enormous variety
that is found among plant fruity

Badly Drawn Poet

Sky white; somersaults going on.
You open up a lemonade stand
and say, "I have pain
down deep in my shoe.
Is there nothing we could do?"

Clouds pass, earth turning—
I feel it, it's my heart that's burning.
You went to buy Tevas
while I stirred the stew.
Is there nothing we could do?

Houses flock the world's surface
as though our lives do have purpose,
but we don't know
what it is, so I ask you,
"Is there nothing we could do?"

I hear a crunch. It's your Honda
bumping into the neighbor's Honda.
Hard to distinguish
false from true:
Is there nothing we could do?

You blow in, arms full of bags,
I picture them as old sea-hags,
and who am I seeing
as their tired queen?
(Is there nothing we could do?)

As from a Dream when One Awakes

I have so ruined myself
reading your bad poems—
ruined, I say, because
my mind has become

a kind of corduroy
of your poems'
awkward lines, the cheek
of my soul imprinted

with their stripes
like a child's cheek
after napping—that when
I arise I will despise

them as fantasies:
how suddenly will they
be rubbed away, until my
soul is supple again!

Garden Shears

She sat
beneath dripping shingles

thinking
visible thoughts

that rose
into interlocking patterns

such as apes
and hydrangeas

she waved
to dispel the smoke

of Lyle's
clove

but it
didn't help because he

was getting
up to leave and exhaled suddenly

a magnificent blue
wave of anxiety settled over her

she reached
up

Violets, Time and Motherhood

One night I lay musing, among violets.
Suddenly it struck me that I was asleep.
In this sleep I saw a number of shapes.
The first of these was a woman weeping.
It might have been a woman sleeping,
or maybe it was a mother praying.
Suddenly it struck me that I was awake,
and I was standing in a room full of doors,
and they were the doors of perception,
and they were not only closed but locked.
I, wakefully, tried to twist each knob.
It struck me that the violets had been
a dream, and that I was probably dead.
So I sat in a chair and hung my head,
not for sorrow, or slumber, but to pray.
And I noticed my children gathered there,
my fruit, my issue, standing together,
and the doors swung open one by one.
One night I lay awake in a music of voices.
It all came to me suddenly, and so I ran
far from the madness, and into a field.
Thorns tore my legs, I panted for air.
I slumped in exhaustion, fell asleep there.
And in my sleeping, began to dream,
and all around me were those violets.

Whispered Jokes

If I'm in such good company, please
explain why I have to keep looking
over my shoulder to see who's not there:

ghost of the staircase, living
room phantasm—whispered jokes,
unheard and ungotten—or maybe not.

I call them the comedians of chance,
and I have discovered that they're
completely cornball. Canned.

They've written routines
in sharpie on their luminous
hands and keep looking down

to see what comes next. My father
used to laud people who know
"what goes where," but I swear,

I don't anymore—it's all up in the air,
half-visible pins twirling end over
end, and I, their ghastly juggler.

So Galactic

My new band name
the Macronauts really
captures the largeness
of what it's like
to be in Los Angeles

where often it feels (
such as at the Edendale
on Saturday) as if you
are very floating the
night full of night

God bless me for now
I have dyed pink hair
and I am ready Lord
I have crapped-up Vans
a studded thunder belt

I am the light of the
light at the center of the
thing that's happening
the most important thing
that's happening currently

Scattered Showers

Just spent some time
poking around the internet.
        It looks like there's a lot of new stuff
going on.

Threw away my Mucky Duck t-shirt.
Didn't fit. Nothing does

except this black polo
and these pleated white chinos.

It looks like there's a lot of stuff getting worn out,
just judging from the dumpster in the alley.

If that's any indication.

So dorky.

Got a note from a friend in Parsippany:
"No thanks." It's OK.
I hear they're having rain out there. So?

There are more than 300 million people in this
fair country, and there's lots of rain everywhere.

Doesn't it all seem *just* like scenery.

Increasing cloudiness late in the day.

Like, I might be driving along, and the
iPod might shuffle to that one Coldplay song:
why now? Here, where the road
    gracefully descends to Steak 'n Shake,
where the trail ends

in

I can't remember. That part is blacked out.
The movie ended without even ending.
I mean, it ended without music or credits:

a fluttering of film and then its snapping
    against the projector.

So I write back: "The feeling is mutual."

    Or that's what I'm of a mind to write,
but I have to assume there are more days ahead.

Robert Keyes

He had neither possessions nor money more than what was
necessary to maintain himself and his wife. Apart from this, he
was a man magnanimous and fearless. —Oswald Tesimond

I wonder where the church calendar and other calendars intersect
such as the war calendar the sex calendar the terror calendar
the farmer's calendar and of course your calendar where your
   class
schedule is and I wonder how the church calendar impacts
as they say in the business world impacts the other calendars
whether it makes the events scheduled on those calendars
more meaningful or maybe creates unwanted complexity and
I wonder whether maybe we should merge them all and stop
calling them calendars but what really piques my interest is the
so called terror calendar its major holidays such as Kristallnacht
and the September Massacres and its averted holidays such as
the Gunpowder Plot I wonder if the botched execution of Robert
Keyes on the last day of January 1606 should be celebrated
he fell to the ground totally conscious was drawn and quartered
in full awareness of what was happening that sounds like
the kind of terror event that would inspire its own traditions
one might even consider moving it over to the church calendar
a kind of middle ground between the birth of Our Savior
and his Death and Resurrection a kind of reminder that unholy
men damned men have terrorized each other and felt shock
but to no avail it availed not his fellowmen the purging of his
gizzards on the block uncommemorated it probably belongs
on the farmer's calendar a reminder of seasons shifting into
seasons of the natural cycle of ups and downs that keep time
going nothing special just a little spring rain another harvest

Accumulata

So you string together a number of moments
and you call it *life*? You say *My life*?
And is there a moment in which you notice
this moment is disconnected from the rest?
So all you have to say in your own defense
is *I believe the lie of temporal continuity*?
And you think you can discern a single story
or several stories threaded together through
the accumulation of moments, like a rainbow
soaring through individual raindrops of time
that makes them something more like *rain*
and less like separate drops? And this being
the case, do you not regard the darker drops,
the desperate drops, the drops of horror,
drops of failure, flat drops, mingled or rather
inexplicably interleaved with the funny,
the sunshiny, the naps, and see, can't you see
that this is your *ordinary*? That these, each
and each, and all, are neither total nor definitive
but are rather, say, *She left*. There is a
moment for it. Or *The last words she spoke*,
which haunts you like a bell whose peal
continues to echo down dreams.
That these, none of them, will damn you.

Acknowledgements

Thanks to the journals in which the following poems first appeared:

1913: "Ad Infinitum," "My Last Duchess," "Tuberculosis Day"
52nd City: "Robert Keyes"
The Atlantic: "Avatar"
Books & Culture: "On the Death of Leslie Nielsen"
Catch Up: "An Enchanted Evening Together," "Loggerheads"
Court Green: "Thomas Hardy the Tank Engine," "Hopkins Palindrome"
Eleven Eleven: "The Clock"
Eleven and a Half: "A Novel"
Esque: "Badly Drawn Poet," "A Horse, Oh Gross"
Gondola: "Risibility Ballad"
H_NGM_N: "Accumulata"
Jacket: "New Movie"
Joyland: "On the Loss of a Finger"
La Petite Zine: "Trees," "Vacation"
Lumberyard: "Song of Myself"
McSweeney's Internet Tendency: "Famous Palindrome"
Mead: "The Silent Life"
Memorious: "Scattered Showers"
No Tell Motel: "Beginning With a Couplet from Jane Kenyon"
The Oxonian Review: "Sergei Rachmaninoff," "Wassily Kandinsky"
Poems-for-All: "Gleff"
Realpoetik: "Starbucks"
Shampoo: "My Chosen Vocation"
Smartish Pace: "1-0"
Sou'wester: "Four Eights"
Tears in the Fence: "Big Face / M4W / Hollywood (Amoeba Music)"
Thermos: "Mesquite Bar Code Squigglies"
Thirteen Blackbirds: "Whispered Jokes"
Tinfish: "Hambone"
Tight: "So This Is Tuesday"
Triggerfish: "As from a Dream when One Awakes"
Yankee Pot Roast: "Two Utah Palindromes"
Zócalo Public Square: "So Galactic," "Howard," "Rhododendron"

With love to Elijah, Natalie and Amelia; editorial props to Stephen Ross,
Chris Davidson, Meghan McEnery, Michael Schiavo and John Drexler; and
in particular recognition of Julie Dill's ongoing encouragement.